Musical Instruments

Piano

By Nick Rebman

level 1
little blue readers

www.littlebluehousebooks.com

Little Blue House is distributed by North Star Editions:
sales@northstareditions.com | 888-417-0195

Produced for Little Blue House by Red Line Editorial.

Photographs ©: Shutterstock Images, cover, 4, 7, 8–9, 10–11, 12–13, 15, 16–17, 19, 21, 24 (top left), 24 (top right), 24 (bottom left), 24 (bottom right); iStockphoto, 22–23

Library of Congress Control Number: 2022910596

ISBN
978-1-64619-700-2 (hardcover)
978-1-64619-732-3 (paperback)
978-1-64619-793-4 (ebook pdf)
978-1-64619-764-4 (hosted ebook)

Printed in the United States of America
Mankato, MN
012023

About the Author

Nick Rebman is a writer and editor who lives in Minnesota. He enjoys reading, walking his dog, and playing rock songs on his drum set.

Table of Contents

Piano

I like to make music.

I play the piano.

I sit on a bench.

I keep my back straight.

bench

The piano has 88 keys.

Some keys are white.

Some keys are black.

key

I put my hands on

the keys.

I press a key.

Each key plays a

different note.

The piano has pedals.
I push them with my feet.
The pedals change how
the notes sound.

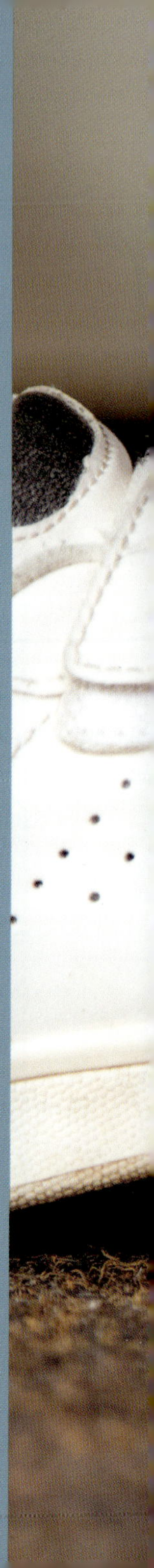

pedal

I sit next to my teacher. She shows me how to play.

teacher

I learn how to read sheet music.
I play slowly at first.

sheet music

I practice every day.

I get better and better.

Soon I can play faster.

I play for other people.

The piano is on a stage.

stage

I play with friends.
We have fun
making music.

Glossary

keys

sheet music

pedals

stage

Index